SPRITZ
COOKIE PRESS RECIPES

Tammy Kaye

RECIPE INDEX

- BLANK PAGE -

SNICKERDOODLE SPRITZ

ingredients

- ½ cup softened butter (1 stick)
- ⅛ teaspoon nutmeg
- 1 tablespoon vanilla extract
- ⅔ cup powdered sugar
- 2 egg yolks
- 2 cups all-purpose flour
- ¼ cup heavy cream
- ¼ cup granulated sugar
- ½ teaspoon cinnamon

directions

1. Heat the oven to 350 F.
2. Line a baking sheet with parchment paper or spray with cooking spray.
3. In a large bowl, cream together butter, nutmeg, vanilla and powdered sugar until creamy and light.
4. Add egg yolks; until combined.
5. Slowly add the flour; mix well.
6. Add cream; beat until combined. The dough should be very soft.
7. Fill cookie press with dough and press cookies 1 inch apart on ungreased baking sheet
8. In a small bowl, combine sugar and cinnamon; sprinkle the mixture over the cookies.
9. Bake 10-12 minutes, or until very lightly browned on the edges.
10. Cool cookies on the baking sheet for 5 minutes before transferring them to cool completely.

ESPRESSO CHOCOLATE SPRITZ

ingredients

Cookies

- 2 ¼ cups all-purpose flour
- 1 tablespoon cocoa
- 1 tablespoon espresso powder
- 1 cup softened unsalted butter
- ¾ cup granulated sugar
- 1 large egg
- 1 teaspoon vanilla extract
- 2 ounces unsweetened baking chocolate melted

Decorating

- 1 ½ – 2 cups melting chocolate chocolate wafers formulated for melting or tempered chocolate
- Sprinkles

directions

1. Preheat oven to 400° F.
2. In a medium bowl, stir together flour, cocoa, and espresso powder.
3. In a large bowl, cream together butter and sugar until light and fluffy.
4. Add egg and vanilla; mix well.
5. Add melted chocolate; mix until combined.
6. Gradually add the flour mixture; mix until combined.
7. Fill cookie press with dough and press cookies 1 inch apart on ungreased baking sheet
8. Bake 7 minutes, or until very lightly browned on the edges.
9. Cool cookies on the baking sheet for 5 minutes before transferring them to cool completely.

Decorating:

Drizzle cookies with melted chocolate and immediately add sprinkles.

- BLANK PAGE -

SIMPLY SPRITZ

ingredients

- 1 cup softened, unsalted butter (2 sticks)
- ¾ cup sugar
- 1 large egg (room temperature)
- 1 teaspoon vanilla extract
- 1 teaspoon almond extract
- 2 ¼ cups flour
- ½ teaspoon salt
- OPTIONAL: sprinkles, chocolate chips, and melted chocolate for decoration

directions

1. Preheat oven to 350°F.
2. Line 2-3 large baking sheets with parchment paper or silicone baking mats.
3. In a large bowl, cream together butter and sugar until smooth.
4. Add egg, vanilla extract, and almond extract, and beat until combined.
5. Slowly beat in the flour and salt until completely combined.
6. Fill cookie press with dough and press cookies 2 inches apart on ungreased baking sheet.
7. Optional, decorate with sprinkles or press chocolate chips into the dough.
8. Bake 7-9 minutes, or until very lightly browned on the edges.
9. Cool cookies on the baking sheet for 5 minutes before transferring them to cool completely.
10. Optional, drizzle with melted chocolate.

JELL-O SPRITZ

ingredients

- 3 ½ cups all-purpose flour
- 1 ½ cups butter (3 Sticks)
- 1 (3-oz.) package jello (any flavor; also adds color to cookies)
- 1 teaspoon baking powder
- 1 cup sugar
- 1 egg
- 1 teaspoon vanilla extract

directions

1. Preheat over to 350ºF.
2. In medium bowl, cream together butter, sugar and jello.
3. Add egg and vanilla; mix well.
4. Slowly blend in flour and baking powder until smooth.
5. Fill cookie press with dough and press cookies 2 inches apart on ungreased baking sheet.
6. Bake at 350º for 11 minutes.
7. Cool cookies on the baking sheet for 5 minutes before transferring them to cool completely.

SHORTBREAD SPRITZ

ingredients

- 2 cups softened butter (4 sticks)
- 1 cup powdered sugar
- 1 teaspoon vanilla extract
- ½ cup cornstarch
- 3 cups all-purpose flour

directions

1. Preheat oven to 350°F with a rack in the middle position.
2. Line baking sheets with parchment paper or silicone mats.
3. In medium bowl, cream together butter, sugar, and vanilla.
4. Slowly blend in cornstarch and flour until dough is light and airy.
5. Fill cookie press with dough and press cookies 1-2 inches apart on ungreased baking sheet.
6. Bake 10-15 minutes, or until very lightly browned on the edges.
7. Cool cookies on the baking sheet for 5 minutes before transferring them to cool completely.

GINGERBREAD SPRITZ

ingredients

- 1 cup softened, unsalted butter (2 sticks)
- ½ cup packed brown sugar
- ½ cup molasses
- 1 egg
- 1 ½ teaspoon vanilla extract
- 3 cups all-purpose flour
- 2 teaspoon ground cinnamon
- 2 teaspoon ground ginger
- ¼ tsp salt
- ¼ tsp ground white pepper (or substitute a pinch of ground black pepper)
- ¼ teaspoon ground cloves

directions

1. In large mixing bowl, cream together butter and brown sugar until smooth.
2. Add molasses, egg, and vanilla extract and mix until combined.
3. In a medium bowl, whisk together flour, cinnamon, ginger, salt, white pepper, and cloves until combined.
4. Slowly add flour mixture to the butter mixture and mix until combined.
5. Place dough on large sheet of plastic wrap and wrap snugly. Refrigerate for 30 minutes.
6. Once chilled, preheat oven to 375°F.
7. Fill cookie press with dough and press cookies 1-2 inches apart on ungreased baking sheet.
8. Bake 5-7 minutes, or until very lightly browned on the edges.
9. Cool cookies on the baking sheet for 5 minutes before transferring them to cool completely.

PUMPKIN SPICE SPRITZ

ingredients

- 1 cup softened butter (2 sticks)
- 1 cup powdered sugar
- 1 large egg
- 1 teaspoon pumpkin spice extract
- 2 ¼ cups all-purpose flour
- 1 teaspoon pumpkin spice
- 1 teaspoon baking powder
- 1 food colouring

directions

1. Preheat oven to 350 degrees.
2. Line a baking sheet with parchment paper or silicone mat.
3. In a mixing bowl, cream together butter and sugar until well combined.
4. Add egg and pumpkin spice extract; beat until combined.
5. In a separate bowl, sift together flour, baking powder, and pumpkin spice.
6. Slowly add flour mixture to the butter mixture and beat until combined.
7. Fill cookie press with dough and press cookies 1 inch apart on ungreased baking sheet.
8. Bake 8 minutes, or until very lightly browned on the edges.
9. Cool cookies on the baking sheet for 2 minutes before transferring them to cool completely.

COFFEE HAZELNUT SPRITZ

ingredients

- ¾ cups softened unsalted butter (1 ½ sticks)
- ½ cup sugar
- ¼ teaspoon salt
- 1 egg
- 2 teaspoons instant espresso granules
- 1 ½ cups all-purpose flour
- ½ cup hazelnut meal

directions

1. Preheat oven to 400ºF.
2. In a large mixing bowl, cream together butter, sugar and salt until light and fluffy.
3. Beat in egg.
4. Stir in the espresso.
5. Stir in the flour and hazelnut meal until combined into a thick dough.
6. Fill cookie press with dough and press cookies 1 inch apart on ungreased baking sheet.
7. Bake 8-10 minutes, or until very lightly browned on the edges.
8. Cool cookies on the baking sheet for 5 minutes before transferring them to cool completely.

CREAM CHEESE SPRITZ

ingredients

- 2 ½ cups all-purpose flour
- ½ teaspoon salt
- 1 cup softened butter (2 sticks)
- 3 ounces softened cream cheese
- 1 cup sugar
- 1 egg yolk
- 1 teaspoon vanilla extract
- ¼ teaspoon lemon extract
- Optional: food coloring
- Optional Decorations: colored sugar, sprinkles, or other decorations

directions

1. Preheat oven to 350 F.
2. In medium bowl, combine salt into flour. Set aside.
3. In a separate medium bowl, cream together butter and cream cheese together until fluffy.
4. Add sugar, egg yolk, vanilla, and lemon or almond extract; Beat.
5. Slowly mix the flour mixture into the butter mixture until combined..
6. OPTIONAL: Divide dough and add food coloring(s); mix well.
7. Fill cookie press with dough and press cookies 1-2 inches apart on ungreased baking sheet.
8. Decorate pressed cookies with optional decorations.
9. Bake 10 to 15 minutes, or until very lightly browned on the edges.
10. Cool cookies on the baking sheet for 5 minutes before transferring them to cool completely.

CHERRY SPRITZ

ingredients

- 3 ½ cups all-purpose flour
- 1 teaspoon baking powder
- 1 ½ cups butter (3 sticks)
- 1 cup sugar
- 1 large egg
- 2 tablespoons milk or cream
- 2 teaspoons cherry flavor
- ½ teaspoon almond extract
- 2 drops red food coloring
- Optional: candies, maraschino cherries, or sprinkles for decoration

directions

1. Preheat the oven to 375 degrees.
2. In a large bowl, whisk the flour and baking powder together. Set aside.
3. Cream together butter and sugar.
4. Add egg, milk or cream, cherry flavor, vanilla extract, almond extract, and beat until combined.
5. Slowly mix in the flour mixture to the creamed mixture.
6. Add enough red food coloring to make a pink dough.
7. Fill cookie press with dough and press cookies 1-2 inches apart on ungreased baking sheet.
8. Optional: Decorate with candies, maraschino cherries, or sprinkles.
9. Bake 6-8 minutes, or until very lightly browned on the edges.
10. Cool cookies on the baking sheet for 5 minutes before transferring them to cool completely.

RASPBERRY ALMOND SPRITZ

ingredients

- ½ cup blanched almonds
- ¾ cup softened butter (1 ½ sticks)
- ½ cup sugar
- 1 egg, room temperature
- 2 tablespoons raspberry preserves
- 1 teaspoon almond extract (vanilla can be used as a substitute)
- ¼ teaspoon salt
- Pink gel food coloring
- 2 ¼ cup all-purpose flour

directions

1. Preheat the oven to 400F.
2. Pulse almonds in a food processor until they turn into a coarse meal, but not too much or you will end up with almond butter!
3. Cream together butter and sugar until fluffy.
4. Mix in the egg, raspberry preserves, almond extract and salt until smooth.
5. Stir in a drop or two of food coloring.
6. Slowly blend in flour and almonds.
7. If the dough feels really sticky, add more flour, 1 tablespoon at a time.
8. Fill cookie press with dough and press cookies 1-2 inches apart on ungreased baking sheet.
9. Bake 8-10 minutes, or until very lightly browned on the edges. .
10. Cool cookies on the baking sheet for 5 minutes before transferring them to cool completely.

- BLANK PAGE -

LEMON SPRITZ

ingredients

- 2 cups all-purpose flour
- ½ teaspoon baking powder
- ¼ teaspoon salt
- ¾ cup softened unsalted butter
  (1 ½ sticks)
- 1 cup sugar
- 2 tablespoon lemon zest
- 1 large egg (room temperature)
- 2 teaspoons lemon juice
- ¼ teaspoon vanilla extract
- OPTIONAL: pink or yellow sanding sugar for decorating

directions

1. Preheat oven to 400F degrees.
2. In a medium bowl, whisk together flour, baking powder, and salt. Set aside.
3. In a large bowl, cream together butter, sugar, and lemon zest until light and fluffy.
4. Beat in egg, lemon juice, and vanilla extract.
5. Slowly add flour mixture until combined.
6. Fill cookie press with dough and press cookies 1 inch apart on ungreased baking sheet.
7. OPTIONAL: Decorate with pink or yellow sanding sugar.
8. Bake 6-8 minutes, or until very lightly browned on the edges.
9. Cool cookies on the baking sheet for 5 minutes before transferring them to cool completely.

PUDDING MIX SPRITZ

ingredients

- 3 ½ cups Flour
- 1 ½ cups softened butter (3 sticks)
- 1 cup Sugar
- 1 package Instant Lemon Jell-o Pudding (3.4 ounce)
- 1 Egg
- 1 Teaspoon Baking Powder
- 1 Teaspoon Vanilla

directions

1. Preheat oven to 400° F.
2. In small bowl, cream together butter, sugar, and pudding package until fluffy.
3. Mix in egg and vanilla.
4. Slowly mix in flour and baking powder until soft, crumbly dough forms.
5. Fill cookie press with dough and press cookies 1 inch apart on ungreased baking sheet.
6. Bake for 5-7 minutes, or until very lightly browned on the edges.
7. Cool cookies on the baking sheet for 5 minutes before transferring them to cool completely.

- BLANK PAGE -

CHOCOLATE PEPPERMINT SPRITZ

ingredients

- ¾ cup softened unsalted butter (1 ½ sticks)
- ¾ cup sugar
- 1 egg
- 1 ½ teaspoons pure vanilla extract
- 1 ½ teaspoons peppermint extract
- ⅛ teaspoon salt
- ¼ cup unsweetened cocoa powder
- 1 ½ cups whole-wheat flour

directions

1. Preheat the oven to 375 degrees F.
2. In a large bowl cream together butter and sugar until well combined.
3. Add egg, vanilla, peppermint, and salt and continue mixing.
4. Slowly add in the cocoa powder and flour until well blended.
5. Fill cookie press with dough and press cookies 1 inch apart on ungreased baking sheet.
6. Bake 10 minutes, or until very lightly browned on the edges.
7. Cool cookies on the baking sheet for 5 minutes before transferring them to cool completely.

CHOCOLATE CANDY CORN SPRITZ

ingredients

- 1 ½ cups softened, unsalted butter (3 sticks)
- 1 cup sugar
- ½ teaspoon salt
- 1 tablespoon vanilla extract
- 2 large eggs at room temperature
- 3 ½ cups all-purpose flour
- ½ cup unsweetened cocoa powder
- Several pieces of candy corn

directions

1. Preheat the oven to 350 degrees.
2. In a large mixing bowl, cream together butter, sugar and salt until light and fluffy.
3. Add vanilla and eggs, beating until combined.
4. Slowly add flour and cocoa powder, beating until combined.
5. Fill cookie press with dough and press cookies 1-2 inches apart on ungreased baking sheet.
6. Bake for 4 minutes.
7. Remove from oven and quickly place candy corn pieces on each cookie.
8. Return to oven and bake for an additional 3 to 4 minutes, or until very lightly browned on the edges.
9. Cool cookies on the baking sheet for 5 minutes before transferring them to cool completely.

BUTTERY GLUTEN FREE SPRITZ

ingredients

- 1 cup softened butter (2 sticks)
- ¾ cup sugar
- 1 large egg
- 2 tsp vanilla extract
- ½ tsp salt
- 2 ¼ cups Gluten Free All Purpose Flour
- Optional: Food Coloring; sprinkles;decorating sugar

directions

1. Preheat oven to 375°
2. Cream together butter & sugar until light and fluffy.
3. Add egg, vanilla, salt, and beat until blended.
4. Slowly add flour and mix until combined.
5. OPTIONAL: Separate dough into multiple small bowls and add a few drops of food coloring to add color.
6. Fill cookie press with dough and press cookies 2 inches apart on ungreased baking sheet.
7. OPTIONAL: Decorate cookies with colored sugar or sprinkles.
8. Bake 8 minutes, or until very lightly browned on the edges.
9. Cool cookies on the baking sheet for 5 minutes before transferring them to cool completely. .

CLASSIC SPRITZ

ingredients

- 3 ½ cups all-purpose flour
- 1 teaspoon baking powder
- 1 ½ cups softened, unsalted butter (3 sticks)
- 1 cup granulated sugar
- 1 egg
- 2 tablespoons milk
- ½ teaspoon almond extract
- 1 teaspoon vanilla extract

directions

1. Preheat oven to 350°F.
2. In a medium sized bowl, combine flour and baking powder.
3. In a separate large bowl, cream together butter and sugar until light and fluffy.
4. Add egg, milk, vanilla and almond extract and mix until combined.
5. Slowly add the flour mixture to butter mixture and beat until combined.
6. Fill cookie press with dough and press cookies 1-2 inches apart on ungreased baking sheet.
7. Bake 10-12 minutes, or until very lightly browned on the edges.
8. Cool cookies on the baking sheet for 2 minutes before transferring them to cool completely.

CINNAMON DULCE de LECHE SPRITZ

ingredients

- 3 ½ cups all purpose flour
- 1 tablespoon ground cinnamon
- 1 teaspoon baking powder
- 1 ½ cups (3 sticks) butter, softened
- 1 cup granulated sugar
- 1 egg
- 2 tablespoons milk
- 1 teaspoon Pure Vanilla Extract
- 1 can (13.4 ounces) dulce de leche

directions

1. Preheat oven to 350ºF.
2. In large bowl, combine flour, cinnamon and baking powder. Set aside.
3. In medium bowl, beat butter and sugar until light and fluffy.
4. Add egg, milk and vanilla; mix well.
5. Slowly add flour mixture to butter mixture, mixing until dough is smooth.
6. Place dough into cookie press and press cookies onto ungreased cookie sheet.
7. Fill cookie press with dough and press cookies 1-2 inches apart on ungreased baking sheet.
8. Bake 10-12 minutes, or until very lightly browned on the edges.
9. Cool cookies on the baking sheet for 2 minutes before transferring them to cool completely.
10. Spread about 1 teaspoon dulce de leche on back of half the cookies and sandwich with remaining cookies.

PISTACHIO SPRITZ

ingredients

- ½ cup pistachios
- 3 ⅓ cups all-purpose flour
- 1 teaspoon baking powder
- 1 ½ cups butter, softened
- 1 cup granulated sugar
- 1 egg
- 2 tablespoons milk
- ½ teaspoon Pure Vanilla Extract
- ½ teaspoon Imitation Almond Extract.
- Green Food Coloring

directions

1. Preheat oven to 350°F.
2. Using food processor, finely ground pistachios (remove any pieces too large to fit through cookie press discs).
3. In medium bowl, combine ground pistachios, flour and baking powder.
4. In large bowl, cream together butter and sugar mix until light and fluffy.
5. Add egg, milk, vanilla and almond extracts and icing color; mix well.
6. Slowly add flour mixture to butter mixture, mix to make a smooth dough.
7. Fill cookie press with dough and press cookies 1-2 inches apart on ungreased baking sheet.
8. Bake 10-12 minutes, or until very lightly browned on the edges.
9. Cool cookies on the baking sheet for 5 minutes before transferring them to cool completely.

SALT & VINEGAR CHIP SPRITZ

ingredients

- 1 cup softened butter (2 sticks)
- ¼ cup granulated sugar
- 1 egg white
- 3 tablespoons malt vinegar
- ½ teaspoon Pure Vanilla Extract
- 2 ¼ cups all-purpose flour
- ½ teaspoon coarse sea salt
- 1 cup potato chips, very finely crushed

directions

1. Preheat oven to 375ºF.
2. In large bowl, cream together butter, sugar and egg white until thoroughly combined.
3. Add vinegar and vanilla; mix well.
4. In small bowl, whisk together flour and salt
5. Slowly add flour mixture to butter mixture and mix well.
6. Add potato chips; mix well.
7. Fill cookie press with dough and press cookies 1-2 inches apart on ungreased baking sheet.
8. Bake 9-11 minutes, or until very lightly browned on the edges.
9. Cool cookies on the baking sheet for 5 minutes before transferring them to cool completely.

CARAMEL MACCHIATO SPRITZ

ingredients

- 1 cup softened, unsalted butter (2 sticks)
- ½ cup granulated sugar
- ¼ teaspoon vanilla extract
- 1 teaspoon instant espresso powder
- 1 tablespoon caramel extract
- 1 large egg, room temperature
- 2 ½ cups all-purpose flour
- ¼ teaspoon salt

directions

1. Preheat oven to 400 degrees F
2. Cream together butter, sugar, vanilla extract, espresso powder, and caramel extract
3. Add egg and mix just until combined.
4. In medium bowl, sift flour and salt. Set aside.
5. Slowly add flour mixture into creamed butter and mix until dough is formed.
6. Fill cookie press with dough and press cookies 1-2 inches apart on ungreased baking sheet.
7. Bake 7-9 minutes, or until very lightly browned on the edges.
8. Cool cookies on the baking sheet for 5 minutes before transferring them to cool completely.

PEANUT BUTTER SPRITZ

ingredients

- 1 cup softened butter (2 sticks)
- 1 cup peanut butter
- 1 cup sugar
- 1 cup brown sugar
- 2 eggs
- 1 teaspoon. vanilla
- 3 cups flour
- 1 teaspoon baking powder
- 1 teaspoon baking soda
- 1 teaspoon salt

directions

1. Preheat oven to 350F.
2. In medium bowl, combine flour, baking powder, baking soda, and salt. Set aside.
3. In large bowl, cream together butter and peanut butter.
4. Add sugar and brown sugar; beat until light and fluffy.
5. Add eggs and vanilla; mix until combined.
6. Slowly add flour mixture to peanut butter mixture; mix until combined.
7. Fill cookie press with dough and press cookies 1-2 inches apart on ungreased baking sheet.
8. Bake 8-12 minutes, or until very lightly browned on the edges.
9. Cool cookies on the baking sheet for 5 minutes before transferring them to cool completely.

CINNAMON SPRITZ

ingredients

- 1 cup softened butter (2 sticks)
- ½ cup + 2 Tablespoons Sugar
- 2 teaspoons vanilla extract
- 1 egg
- 2-½ cups all-purpose flour
- 1 Tablespoon ground cinnamon
- ½ teaspoon salt

directions

1. Preheat over to 375F.
2. Cream together butter and sugar until well blended.
3. Slowly add vanilla extract and egg; Mix until well blended.
4. In a separate bowl, mix flour, ground cinnamon, and salt.
5. Slowly add flour mixture into butter mixture; mix until fully incorporated.
6. Fill cookie press with dough and press cookies 1-2 inches apart on ungreased baking sheet.
7. Bake 6-8 minutes, or until very lightly browned on the edges.
8. Cool cookies on the baking sheet for 5 minutes before transferring them to cool completely.

WHITE CHOCOLATE SPRITZ

ingredients

- 2 oz white chocolate baking bar or white chips
- ¾ cup softened butter (1 ½ sticks)
- ½ cup sugar
- ½ teaspoon salt-(omit if using salted butter)
- 1 egg
- 2 teaspoon vanilla
- 2 ½ cup flour
- Candy decorations or sprinkles

directions

1. Preheat oven to 350F.
2. Melt white chocolate in microwave, stir and set aside.
3. Cream together butter, sugar and salt until creamy.
4. Add egg and vanilla, mix until combined.
5. Add melted chocolate, mix until combined.
6. Slowly add in flour, mix until combined.
7. Fill cookie press with dough and press cookies 1-2 inches apart on ungreased baking sheet.
8. Bake 10 minutes, or until very lightly browned on the edges.
9. Cool cookies on the baking sheet for 5 minutes before transferring them to cool completely.

- BLANK PAGE -

HARVEST SPICE SPRITZ

ingredients

- 1 cup softened butter (2 sticks)
- ¾ cup sugar
- ½ cup cream cheese
- ¾ teaspoon salt
- 2 teaspoons vanilla extract
- 1 ½ teaspoons ground cinnamon
- 1 teaspoon ground cardamom
- ¼ teaspoon ground nutmeg
- ⅛ teaspoon ground allspice or ground clove
- 1 large egg yolk
- 2 ½ cups Flour
- OPTIONAL: colored sugar for decorations

directions

1. Preheat oven 375°F.
2. Cream together butter, sugar, cream cheese, salt, vanilla, cinnamon, cardamom, nutmeg, allspice (or clove).
3. Beat in the egg yolk.
4. Slowly mix in the flour.
5. Fill cookie press with dough and press cookies 1-2 inches apart on ungreased baking sheet.
6. OPTIONAL: Top with colored sugar.
7. Bake 8 to 10 minutes, or until very lightly browned on the edges.
8. Cool cookies on the baking sheet for 5 minutes before transferring them to cool completely. .

- BLANK PAGE -

CHAI SPICE SPRITZ

ingredients

- 3 ½ cups all-purpose flour
- 1 teaspoon baking powder
- 1 ½ teaspoon ground cardamom
- 1 ½ teaspoon ground cinnamon
- ½ teaspoon ground ginger
- ¼ teaspoon ground cloves
- ¼ teaspoon ground nutmeg
- ¼ teaspoon salt
- 1 ½ cups softened, unsalted butter
  (3 sticks)
- 1 cup sugar
- 1 large egg
- 2 tablespoons milk
- 1 teaspoon vanilla extract

directions

1. Preheat oven to 350 degrees F.
2. Line a large cookie sheet with a baking mat or parchment paper.
3. In a medium bowl, stir together flour, baking powder, cardamon, cinnamon, ginger, cloves, nutmeg, and salt. Set aside.
4. In a large bowl, cream together butter and sugar until well-combined.
5. Beat in the egg, milk, and vanilla.
6. Slowly add the flour mixture to the butter mixture and mix until combined.
7. Fill cookie press with dough and press cookies 1-2 inches apart on ungreased baking sheet.
8. Bake 10 minutes, or until very lightly browned on the edges.
9. Cool cookies on the baking sheet for 5 minutes before transferring them to cool completely.

APPLE BUTTER SPRITZ

ingredients

- ½ cup apple butter
- ½ cup softened butter (1 stick)
- 1 cup sugar
- 1 egg yolk
- 1 teaspoon Pure Vanilla Extract
- ¾ teaspoon cinnamon
- 2 ½ cups all-purpose flour

directions

1. Preheat oven 350°F.
2. In mixing bowl, cream together apple butter, butter and sugar until light and fluffy.
3. Add egg yolk, vanilla, cinnamon and mix until combined
4. Slowly mix in flour until blended.
5. Fill cookie press with dough and press cookies 1-2 inches apart on ungreased baking sheet.
6. Bake 10-12 minutes, or until very lightly browned on the edges.
7. Cool cookies on the baking sheet for 2 minutes before transferring them to cool completely.

- BLANK PAGE -

Made in the USA
Las Vegas, NV
02 December 2024

13209431R00033